Christianity

The Unadulterated

Truth

Christianity
The Unadulterated Truth

by Andrea Chambers

Christianity The
Unadulterated Truth
By Andrea Chambers
Copyright 2014
By
Library of Congress

No part of this book may be used or reproduced in any manner whatsoever without written permission of the publisher except brief quotations embodied in critical articles or reviews or from the quotations from Bible.

Scripture quotations used in this book are from the Holy Bible, King James Version (KJV).

Dedication and Memory

I'm dedicating this book to two important people who are the reason that I am who I am today in the Lord, which is a strong black woman that stands for righteousness, truth and justice for all men and women.

The late Bishop Thomas N. Conway was my spiritual father in the Lord, who taught me how to serve the Lord and to pursue the truth and live the truth—he always said if you make a mistake get up and keep moving because you won't be the first to make a mistake and you won't be the last—that was told to me when I was young in the Lord—he was known to get people delivered and filled with God's Holy Ghost while calling on the name of *Jesus*, I was the last member to get the Holy Ghost--he was a great man that never got his dues-but he didn't let that stop him from serving God to the end.

Then there was my late husband, Prophet, and Elder Roger Chambers, who had great power with God. So many times, he would tell me of new inventions that years later would come out. He did that regularly. He could tell when a woman was pregnant the day she conceived. He prophesied his own death, he told me on the day we got married after we had been married for a few hours that he wasn't going to live to his 40th birthday and it came to pass—he had a massive heart attack while he was in the hospital for something else and he was 39 years-old. His last prophecy was to me that Satan was coming after me next and I'll go through like never before and as he said I started suffering that night with a seizure and it's been one hardship after another but I've been standing. I've backed-up at one point but I came back to myself and the majority of my life I've been with God and remain in the truth with God and Jesus as my guide. My late husband would get on the drums and played those drums in power, when he played the drums everyone would be dancing in the spirit. God's anointment was all over him. He would prophesy to people and stick with them until they get delivered and not one time did, he ask for money like so many of these prophets do today, and he served God to the end.

I learned from both of them that to serve God and stand for the truth will be a lonely, hard way because so many times people don't want the truth and it makes the person bringing it not liked, but it is worth it every step of the way because so long as you bring the truth Heaven will get to be your home in the end. So many times, we put people in Heaven and that is not our jobs to do but what I can say if anybody had a chance for Heaven to be their home it would be the both of them because I was right there with both of them until their deaths.

Acknowledgement

To my daughter Helen who is more like me then I care to admit while having a combination of her father's ways and looks, who has a beautiful heart and who is also very smart and has become a woman that I'm very proud of. She has 4 beautiful children that I won't mention names but I'll tell you a little about them—the oldest is a male, who is very respectful and loving who I am also proud of, then there is the one next to the oldest who is a female that is now in college and got her driver's license before going to college who I am also proud of, she is very bright and she has old wisdom to her, then there is the next one who is also a female who is in high school and had a recent birthday, I just can't believe that she's 15 years old, they grow so fast, she is very inquisitive and fashion is her gift every since she was a little toddler she would fix things to make them look better, with her clothes or in the house and I'm very proud of her as well, and the last child is a boy who looks just like his father, he is smart and truthful, he thinks like a man, for a child he has many qualities of a man, the way he thinks and he's not afraid to tell you the truth no matter who you are, if you're wrong about something he will say it and he's very respectful when doing it and I'm very proud of him too.

My daughter did a good job of raising her children they're very respectful, giving, with good hearts and I can't ask for any more in my daughter and my grandchildren.

I have a son named Maurice who passed away at a very young age, he wasn't my natural son but I loved as if he was. He had a beautiful heart. He just loved everybody. He was a good child never giving any trouble. If he did bad things, I never seen it. He was always respectful, very smart, he got that from his mother she is a very smart woman and his dad was a smart man. I miss him so much and I have nothing but good memories of him that I will always cherish.

I have two more sons' that weren't my natural sons, one I raised the other I didn't. The one that I raised his name is Roger, he was named after his father, my late husband. He was quite like his dad, good in school, loved to play with his sister, my daughter, they did everything together, even told their teachers that they were twins. The teachers asked me how can they be twins their birthdates are two weeks apart. I explained that they weren't twins but that's how close they were. And just to think now he has three children of his own two girls and a boy. One of the girls kept me on my knees she almost didn't make it when she was born but she was doing much better the last time I saw her. My other son Lamont, I didn't raise but when he came around, he was always respectful and causing no trouble at least that I could see, when I last saw him, he had two girls and two boys. I also have two daughters that are not my natural daughters Vanessa and Lisa. Vanessa stayed with us for a while when she was a young teenager we always got along fine and later she had a son, who I would play games with him over the phone and Lisa has two girls pretty like their mother. I miss my grandchildren and don't know if I have more because my step children haven't seen me for years nor brought any of my grandchildren to see me, so that's part of pain that I deal with.

I'm grateful that my mother is yet in the land of the living and I just love her so much—she is a strong woman that has been through a lot but in looking at her you would never know it she just doesn't look her age. I lost my father years ago, he died young. I'm the oldest of three brothers and one sister. And I've loved them all as not only my siblings but as my children. I never thought it was a chore to help take care of them. While most kids wanted to play, I wanted to take care of my sisters and brothers. That was fun for me. Now they all have children except one of my brothers and some even have grandchildren like me. I have a nephew that was murdered and that was hard on all of us, he had just turned 18. I miss him so much he was a Scorpio like me, we had so much in common except he was very talented and I'm not as talented. This is my family that I love very much and stay on my knees for—it's worth it.

Published in the United States of America.

CONTENTS

Dedication and Memory iii

Acknowledgement v

Introduction xi

Chapter I Does Religion lead us to God 1

> ➤ Ten Commandments 4
> ➤ Adam and Eve 5
> ➤ Noah 8
> ➤ Religion (Judaism/Christianity) 9
> ➤ Catholic Church 13
> ➤ One religion and One Faith 19

Chapter II True Servant of God through His Son 26

Chapter III Faith of the Fifth Kingdom 29

Chapter IV Fifth Kingdom of today's society 31

Chapter V Of the Fifth Kingdom--Where do you fit in? 37

> ◆ Where does the Catholic Church fit in? 39
> ◆ Trinity as apposed to Godhead 42

- ♦ Ten Commandments vs. Ceremonial Laws 43
- ♦ Melchizedec Priesthood 50
- ♦ Muslims 52
- ♦ Blood Stained America 59
- ♦ Homosexuality 61
- ♦ Hitler and Jews 67
- ♦ Men vs. Women's place in the Lord 76
- ♦ Existence of Angels 81
- ♦ Search for the Truth 84
- ♦ Follow Tradition or Truth 87

About the Author 91

Introduction

First, I would like you to pray before you begin reading this book. Ask God to lead you as you read and not just for this book but for everything in your life. Prayer should always come first it is what our Lord and Savior Jesus Christ did. If you don't know what to pray, just ask God to show you the truth. Also, if you are trying to get to know God or do know Him but just want a closer walk with Him, you need to understand that it takes time for you to get to know God for yourself, so just bear in mind that God loves you, and will be patient with you, and wants you to know the truth or you would not have received this book.

Next, in these present times, truth doesn't seem to prevail anymore. There are so many people dying because we are living in the last and evil days and Jesus will return soon. Yet, there is nothing to fear, if you are in the truth which is the main reason that I wrote this book. Then there will be those that will look at that statement and say if we don't go your way than we should fear; and, the answer to that is that I don't claim to be the only truth but I am a part of the truth that you should at least consider. As Noah was ignored, neither should I nor anyone else that God has shown the truth be ignored. All I can say is that truth convicts the heart and if you truly want Heaven to be your home in the end, then open your heart and mind, not just for what I have to say but for whoever comes to you in God's name. Does that mean that everyone that comes in God's name speak the truth? No. But as I've found out for myself, all you need to do is consider what is said and God will touch your heart and open up your understanding to the truth. Yet, one catch to that is that you truly need to seek for the truth and not for those things that are comfortable to you because it is a way that you have been taught.

As a result, I would like to present you with some questions to reflect upon that which will be addressed in this book and they are: Is there any religion that leads us to the Living God and His Son? Who is truly a servant of the Living God and His Son? What faith is of the fifth Kingdom that Daniel spoke of? What part do we play in society today that places us in the fifth Kingdom? When God's Son returns to establish His Kingdom where will you fit in?

Importantly, I'm entering this section because of what a Muslim friend of mine told me after reading my book. He said that I need to look inside out before I write about Muslims, and I took that advice in writing everything in this book. I'm not going to change the truth in this book because the truth is the truth; however, one thing that I can do, is tell the truth with compassion. In this book, I speak about what is wrong with the Muslim faith but I need to also state where they are right. Muslims pray a mandatory five times a day and there are many that pray more than five times per day as well. They faithfully teach their children the Quran which is extremely important because we should raise our children in our belief. There is a day of celebration where food and drinks are free for everyone in the country; you don't pay for food at any of the restaurants. I have met Muslims with beautiful hearts that want peace and love among their fellow man; therefore, they show peace and love by example and these are just some of the right things among many.

Equally important, are the Christians that are under the Catholic faith. Even though I speak the truth about Catholicism, I must add that I have seen and known loving spirits and beautiful hearts that so many protestants need to have, and showing the love of God by dedicating their heart and soul helping their fellow man and possess true humbleness while raising their children to do the same; truly, these attributes are of great price to the Living God.

Furthermore, this book shows the truth and the truth can be hard, but hard will make you strong and able to stand what things Satan shall throw your way to try and knock you out of your place for Heaven. I feel that this book is important because it shows the truth where so many **do not**. Do I say that my way is the only way? No. However, I do say that the truth is the only way. Not my way vs. your way or this way vs. that way but rather the truth that has stood through time, is standing now, and will stand when all is gone. The truth that was here long before, I, Andrea, came to be, or any of us, here, in this present time, or any kind of future time truth shall endure when everything else fails, truth shall still prevail.

<<<<<<< *Does Religion lead us to God?* >>>>>>>

There is only one true God and the Creator of all things and He has a Son. We, as a society, have become too complacent with many different faiths within one religion, claiming the same God. Not to mention the many different religions claiming that they are the way to God. Therefore, we must look at religion and the basis of religion.

Henceforth, religion, itself does not lead us to God but rather it is the truth that leads us to God. Within religion, there are certain sets of rules that govern our beliefs and it is these rules that set a Methodist apart from a Baptist and a Baptist apart from a Pentecostal and a Pentecostal apart from a Catholic, a Catholic apart from a Seventh-day Adventist and a Seventh-day Adventist apart from a Jehovah's Witness, and a Jehovah's Witness apart from a Mormon, Orthodox and Unorthodox and so on and so forth, yet all claim Christianity. Not to mention the different religions that claim their way is the way to God as Judaism, Islam, Buddhism, Hinduism, Sikhism,

Taoism, Deism, Gnosticism, Rastafari, Scientology, and so on and so forth. Certainly, the answer to these questions should come to mind and the questions are--Is *Jesus* your Savior? Are the rules that govern your church the same rules that *Jesus* placed for us all? The answer should be yes to both, if not, then they need to be, and if so, then why are there so many different faiths within the Christian community.

There is only one true God, the Creator of all things and He has a Son, *Jesus* Christ, our Messiah who gave us explicit instructions as to how to walk as His true followers. Therefore, why don't we as Christians walk in the same straight and narrow way that leads us to Him? For broad is the way that leads us to destruction. We must look within ourselves for the truth and must see within ourselves what makes sense and what does not make sense. The answer is within, as you read this book or any book, really anything in life, pray first and ask God to lead you, and whether something is right or wrong, God will show you.

It is important to note that there is only one God; the Father of us all and He has a Son, *Jesus* Christ, who was sent that the world through Him, might be saved. We must keep in mind and heart that Satan is the father of lies and he is full of deceit. The dictionary defines deceive as "*To cause to believe what is false or disbelieve what is true.*" In defining deceit, I show you plainly that Satan does not want anyone to be in the truth. Satan will either have you believe false doctrine or not believe doctrine that is true, either way your soul is lost and that is his goal--to capture your soul. Therefore, it is important for us to understand religion and its foundation. The foundation of religion is to worship God while here on Earth until our time comes to be with Him in Heaven. There are a set of rules that we are to go by within religion that governs our faith; but our faith and our religion should be all one and the same.

Israel's God is our God. Yet, before He chose Israel, He created Adam and Eve, male and female created He them, and religion came from those that walked with God and kept His Commandments. Therefore, we who are the Gentiles have been engrafted into the fold that through Jesus Christ, the whole world might be saved.

➤ Ten Commandments

Just as important, the Ten Commandments were before God wrote them for the children of Israel by His finger when He gave them to His servant, Moses. The Ten Commandments were before time began, had they not been, then Lucifer known as the Morning Star would have never been thrown out of Heaven. There never would have been a reason for war to take place in Heaven between God's Holy Angels and Lucifer and the third part of Angels that sided with him; however, because he broke the first Commandment and the pride of his beauty and power made him to believe that he was equal to God, making himself a god, got him and the Angels that followed him thrown out of Heaven.

> *Isaiah 14: 12-15; How art thou fallen from heaven, O Lucifer, son of the morning! How art thou cut down to the ground, which didst*

weaken the nations! **13.** *For thou hast said in thine heart, I will ascend into heaven, I will exalt my throne above the stars of God: I will sit also upon the mount of the congregation, in the sides of the north:* **14.** *I will ascend above the heights of the clouds; I will be like the most High.* **15.** *Yet thou shalt be brought down to hell, to the sides of the pit.*

> **Adam and Eve**

Also, we must remember that Satan is a power and that he is the father of lies and all that is evil. His first deceit among men was to trick the weaker vessel and that was Eve.

> **Genesis 3:1;** *Now the serpent was more subtle than any beast of the field which the Lord God had made. And he said unto the woman, Yea, hath God said, Ye shall not eat of every tree of the garden?*

So, Eve ate the forbidden fruit and then gave it unto her husband and he did eat and their eyes were opened, knowing good and evil. As a result, Satan caused death to fall upon man; from the dust we came, unto the dust we shall return. Moreover, we must keep in mind that Satan has been fighting against God ever since over souls, even as the book of Job shows us:

> ***Job1: 6;*** *Now there was a day when the sons of God came to present themselves before the Lord, and Satan came also among them.*

Thus, Satan fights what he does not have not what he already controls, and this is Spiritual warfare. Even though there is a constant fight while here on Earth until our final resting place, if we choose God. God keeps us while here on Earth and always makes a way for us to escape. If we keep this in mind, we will have half of the battle won, and the other half will be to serve God in faith whole-heartedly for Heaven to be our Home in the end by seeing the end like Job.

> ***Job 42:10;** And the Lord turned the captivity of Job, when he prayed for his friends: also, the Lord gave Job twice as much as he had before.*
> ***Job 42:16-17;** After this lived Job a hundred and forty years, and saw his sons, and his sons' sons, even four generations. **17.** So Job died, being old and full of days.*

As a matter of fact, we need to take a closer look at the religious realm. Was religion mentioned when Enoch walked with God and walked so strongly with God that he did not see death but was taken up in glory?

> ***Genesis 5:21-24;** And Enoch lived sixty and five years, and begat Methuselah: **22.** And Enoch walked with God after he begat Methuselah three hundred years, and begat sons and daughters: **23.** And all the days of Enoch were three hundred sixty and five years: **24.** And*

> *Enoch walked with God: and he was not: for God took him.*

- **Noah**

Was religion mentioned when Noah found grace in the eyes of the Lord and eight souls were saved along with animals when God destroyed the inhabitants of the World?

> ***Genesis 6:7-8;*** *And the Lord said, I will destroy man whom I have created from the face of the earth; both man, and beast, and the creeping thing, and the fowls of the air; for it repenteth me that I have made them.* ***8.*** *But Noah found grace in the eyes of the Lord.*

Hence, God rained upon the Earth forty days and forty nights until all humans and animals were killed except for Noah and His family and the animals that he had on the Ark that God had him build. God made a covenant with Noah that He will place a rainbow in the sky whenever it rains to show that He will not destroy the world with water ever again.

> *Genesis 9: 8-9; And God spake unto Noah, and to his sons with him, saying, 9. And I, behold, I establish my covenant with you, and with your seed after you; Genesis 9:18-19; And the sons of Noah that went forth of the ark were Shem, and Ham, and Japheth: and Ham is the father of Canaan. 19. These are the three sons of Noah: and of them was the whole earth overspread.*

- **Religion (Judaism/Christianity)**

Abram is a descendent of Shem, but was religion mentioned when he served God with so strong a faith that he became Abraham, the father of many nations?

> *Genesis 17:5; Neither shall thy name any more be called Abram, but thy name shall be Abraham; for a father of many nations have I made thee. Genesis 18:18; Seeing that Abraham shall surely become a great and mighty nation, and all the nations of the earth shall be blessed in him?*

And what of Isaac, Abraham and Sarah's promised child, who served and walked with God and was the father of Esau and Jacob? And what of Jacob, Isaac's son who walked before God and wrestled with the Angel until he was blessed and his name was changed to Israel?

> ***Genesis 35:10;*** *And God said unto him, thy name is Jacob: thy name shall not be called any more Jacob, but Israel shall be thy name: and he called his name, Israel.*

These were all before Israel went into the Babylonian captivity where the word Judaism sprung from.

Therefore, before Judaism, people just walked with God without a religious body or name, then later came Judaism, then Christianity. It is again, important to note that our religion and our faith should be one and the same which is to be like Christ. Knowing that throughout the Old Testament Christ was prophesied to come, then when He came, He was rejected of His own, the Jews, but in that, we, the Gentiles should rejoice and be happy and not hate the Jews but love them because had they not rejected

Christ, we, the Gentiles would never have had a chance to be engrafted in for Heaven. Now, both the Jew and the Gentile that serve the Living God through *Jesus* Christ, His Son by way of the Holy Ghost are all called Christians.

> ***Acts 11:26;*** *And when he had found him, he brought him unto Antioch. And it came to pass, that a whole year they assembled themselves with the church, and taught much people. And the disciples were called Christians first in Antioch.*

Christianity is truly more than just a religion and a faith. It is also a way of life, meaning to be Christ–like. And to be Christ–like is to serve God as Christ served Him, and to be like–minded as Christ. To be perfect as our Father which art in Heaven is perfect as Christ instructed us to be.

> ***Matthew 5:48;*** *Be ye therefore perfect, even as your Father which is in heaven is perfect.*

In short, to have perfect love, and this perfection comes from only one way for there is one Lord, one faith, one baptism, and the Father of us all.

*Ephesians 4:5-6; One Lord, one faith, one baptism, **6.** One God and Father of all, who is above all, and through all, and in you all.*

I heard a preacher say that we are all different branches on the same tree. And when I heard that, I was angry and hurt at the same time because Satan truly is the father of lies and all that is evil. There is only one way to God. Only one way is right and all the other ways are wrong. And this is where arguments start, even wars and killings. But the truth is that only Judgment Day will tell if your name is written in the Book of Life or not; therefore, it behooves us to weigh all Spiritual things carefully for the sake of our soul.

> ***Catholic Church***

Most importantly, we must look at a man by the name of Constantine, he was a Roman Emperor that was supposed to have converted from Rome's polytheistic system, meaning worshiping more than one god, to a monotheistic system, meaning to worship one God. Yet, truly, he kept to a polytheistic system by bringing forth Trinity. Three separate entities, instead of the one Godhead as Apostle Paul explained it. ***Romans 1:20; For the invisible things of him from the creation of the world are clearly seen, being understood by the things that are made, even his eternal power and Godhead; so that they are without excuse.*** Most important, so many Christians go with Trinity because naturally it makes sense but there is **<u>no Bible</u>** to backup Trinity but there is Bible for Godhead which was Apostle Paul's way of explaining to us something that is spiritual and will not naturally, make sense. In addition, if you look at it this way, *Jesus* said when you see Him you see the Father and when He goes back to the Father, He will send us a comforter, which is the Holy

Ghost, and this is the one Godhead. Constantine may have stopped the extremely severe bloody killings and persecutions but he had his personal agenda, which was not a good one for God's true Christians. There is a saying which goes this way, "if you can't beat them, join them" and if you join them and conform their system to your beliefs, you do far more damage than fighting people that gladly and willingly die for their beliefs. Because the true Christians had no fear of death and as they were being killed out, they were converting Romans and true Christianity was spreading among the Romans. He was the worst thing to happen to Christianity and so was the beginning of change for Christianity with the Edict of Milan, which was supposedly introduced to put an end to persecution, yet at what cost; then, the Council of Nicene, which brought about so many creeds within the Christian Community that are not of the Living God. It was better when the Romans were killing the Christians because at least, there were the Christians and the non-Christians. Those that died for Christ sake and those that killed them; however, now, after Constantine so many different branches, of faith, have sprung up within the Christian Community and this should not be. Furthermore, there were many killings by order of the Roman Catholic Church to those that would not conform; and people look at this bloody history and say Christians fighting Christians, when in reality it was Rome still persecuting Christians under the guise of Christianity.

Constantine did not convert to Christianity, rather he conformed so much of Christianity into a falsehood by the works of Satan, himself. Furthermore, our eyes have been blinded for a season, but now is time to awaken because soon, our Lord will be coming back for us, who are His. I want you to look and see plainly the following truth for yourselves:

Do you believe that God's day of rest is Sunday? Constantine.

Do you believe or do you know of Easter as Resurrection time? Constantine.

Do you believe Jesus rose on Sunday morning? Constantine.

Do you believe in Ash Wednesday? Constantine.

Do you believe that Passover and Easter are one and at the same time? Constantine.

Do you believe or know of Communion, especially more than once per year? Constantine.

Do you believe the Sabbath was changed to Sunday by Apostle Paul? Constantine.

Do you believe that a man can forgive you for your sins? Constantine.

Do you believe that Mary, the mother of Jesus should be prayed to? Constantine.

Do you believe that the church should give consent as to who can be a saint? Constantine.

Do you believe that Jesus was born in the winter? Constantine.

Do you believe there were three wise men? Constantine.

Do you believe in Christmas? Constantine.

Do you know that Pagan holidays replaced Christian days? Constantine.

Do you know there is no such thing as Trinity? Constantine.

Do you know that God the Father, God the Son, God the Holy Ghost, all make one Godhead and not three totally separate Triune or Trinity? Constantine.

There is so much more that I can go into but this is enough to give you an idea of what damage Constantine has done to the Christian World. There are those who would say many of the things you blame on Constantine happened before his time and long after his death, but in that I must say Emperor Constantine who conformed Christianity to fit true Roman beliefs which fit him instead of becoming a true Christian. He brought in beliefs that were before him, during his time, and for future changes by setting up the Nicene Creed from the Council of Nicaea. You must understand that they were not only losing the fight against Jewish Christians and Greek and other Christians who were willing to die for Christ but they were losing their own Romans as well to what they called a Sect of Christ. The Roman Christians were willing to deny Rome and die for Christ and they were growing in number as well as the Greek Christians and other Gentile Christians.

So Emperor Constantine did a deed that came from no one but Satan, he joined and conformed until when people mention Christianity even in religious secular or non-secular classes the Catholic faith is a primary figure of the Christian movement as if he was a big part of moving Christianity forward, which is a total lie and not at all the truth; therefore, where he may not have been, directly responsible for every wrong thing that has come upon true Christianity he is most definitely indirectly responsible for all that he directly initiated as change. Yet, God foresaw what was to come, that is why Daniel prophesied that they think to change times and laws but do not.

> ***Daniel 7:25;*** *And he shall speak great words against the most High, and shall wear out the*

saints of the most High, and think to change times and laws: and they shall be given into his hand until a time and times and the dividing of time.

➤ *One Religion and One Faith*

What has happened is that Satan has provided a grand diversity of faiths within the same religion so that the truth can be lost. We, as Christians should be of one faith and one religion leading us to the one God, who has one Son and it is that simple.

It is now time for God's chosen to arise out of the miry clay and place our feet on Holy ground, simply meaning it is time for the full truth to emerge, for our Messiah is soon to return and we need to be ready. Jesus is looking for a church without a spot or a wrinkle, meaning to be reborn. You must be baptized of the water and of the Spirit.

It is so important to keep in mind that you have a soul that will live for eternity. The question is, do you want to live that eternity in Joy and Peace? Or do you want to live that eternity in agony and torment? We have only two choices; therefore, we must make our choice. There are people that do evil deeds and say they do not mind going to Hell, and there are people who just conclude that as long as they don't bother anyone, they aren't bad at all. These are the tricks of Satan. He has people headed for the Lake of Fire and he, himself, doesn't want to go there.

Dear children, listen to me carefully. This earth is going to become the Lake of Fire that shall burn for eternity, for it will be an unquenchable fire, and there will be weeping and gnashing of teeth, for the tremendous pain that will last for eternity. Do, listen to me; the Lake of Fire is not the place that you want to end up in. There are so many people that say God will not have a place of forever torment. Yet the book of Revelation tells us different. Furthermore, it is better to be safe and live right and find in the end that you didn't need to do something than to live as if there is no Hell and to find out in the end that you were wrong.

When Jesus comes back for His chosen, all I can say is that you want to be ready. It is an easy thing to do. Some things that are required of you may seem difficult but it's not. When you are new in the Lord, He gives you time to convert, for He is patient, and He is so very good and loving. The more you get to know Him for yourself, the more you will find yourself wanting to do things different and to just be a whole new person. For those of you that have been around awhile as myself, you already have the understanding of just how good God is, that is why He is bringing this truth now, so that we all can escape from the hands of Satan, and be in God's will.

We must come to the truth and recognize that Satan is a power, he is very powerful, and he'll have you do things that you didn't think that you were capable of doing. Satan is forceful, especially, when he wants you to do wrong. He is the tempter. Yet, we must keep in mind that God is all POWER, there is none greater than Him. God can keep you above and take you through anything that Satan has in store for you. And when you call on the name of Jesus, Satan and all his demons must flee. It is also important to know that God never let us be tempted above what we are able to bear. WE HAVE GOD'S PROTECTION, WE HAVE JESUS DELIVERENCE, WE HAVE THE HOST OF HEAVENLY ANGELS FIGHTING FOR US, AND THE BLESSED HOLYGHOST WAS SENT AS A COMFORT FOR US, just know that to be in God is to be forever blessed. For God will bless us here on Earth and give us the desires of our heart and keep us blessed until Heaven becomes our Home, where we will be forever full of JOY.

Further, as I have stated earlier that there should be one faith in the Christian Community. I am not stating that if there is one religion and one faith then there should only be one church. It is important that we do not forget to assemble ourselves together. The Church is extremely important and should not be left out. Yet, we need to look at the schisms within the Churches, to be able to better understand how the Church of the Living God in Jesus name should run, when searching for true salvation.

We should be of one religion and one faith and that should be true Christianity. So many people wonder why I haven't found a church home yet. I fellowshipped but I've not found a church home but it is a good thing to be a part of a church because the bible says for us to come together but one main thing is that I haven't found a true Christian church that don't follow any of the Catholic ways. Even Seventh Day Adventist are divided in believing in Christmas celebration and Easter and Easter Sunday all of Catholic beliefs and most importantly they don't believe in Hell. There are quite amount of people who believe that God would not have a Hell a place of forever torment because He is the God of Love. While it is true that GOD and LOVE are synonymous GOD is also JUST. Let me ask a question to those of you who don't believe that God would have a place of forever torment—wouldn't it be just to take a serial killer who without feeling killed person after person and give them forever torment for what they've done? Wouldn't it be just to take a person that has suffered hurts and pain, even death because they believe in Christ to get to live with Him in Heaven in the end where they'll be no more tears? Both ways are just. Further, who are we as weak humans to say what is and what isn't just about God.

Some will look at the Old Testament when God told Israel to wipe out a whole nation of people. That God was wrong. But all I know is that the Earth is His and all of us in it. If He says remove a Nation of people, only He can and the Nations that He had Israel remove where people that did not serve Him but served idols which is nothing but serving Satan and his Demons. There are those that saying they're killing in the name of God. All I know is it better be Israel's God which is all our God if not you're doing the deed of Satan and Hell will get to be your Home in the end. Another important thing to mention about Hell is that I'd rather live in faith and belief and to do what God requires of me and not to do the wrong things in life so that Hell doesn't get to be my home and I'd rather hear God say to me daughter all that you've done in life wasn't necessary but Heaven gets to be your Home than for Him to say to me when I showed you and told you the right things to do and you didn't feel they were necessary but they were so now depart from Me for I know you not and Hell gets to be your Home. Furthermore, Seventh Day Adventist still hold to Ellen White's prophecy of *Jesus* coming which anyone who reads the bible would know that *Jesus* said no one would know not even Him but only the Father, yet they still hold to that prophecy. Therefore, while I'm a Christian that believes in the Sabbath, I am most definitely not a Seventh Day Adventist. An important verse to understand for all Christians is **I Corinthians 1:10** Now I beseech you, brethren, by the name of our Lord *Jesus* Christ, that ye all speak the same thing, and that there be no divisions among you; but that ye be perfectly joined together in the same mind and in the same judgement.

<<<<   *True Servant of God through His Son*   >>>>

To be a follower of God we must be a follower of His Son, *Jesus* Christ. We must also remember that Satan is the father of lies and is full of deceit; therefore, as true servants of the Living God we must remain mindful and always search for the truth from the heart and this is for the beginner in Christ to a seasoned Christian. Our heart will show us the truth, meaning you will be able to feel if something is right or wrong, even if you don't completely understand it. ***I John 3:20-21;*** *For if our heart condemn us, God is greater than our heart, and knoweth all things.* ***21.*** *Beloved, if our heart condemn us not, then have we confidence toward God.*

Most importantly, the only way that these versus work is that you are honest with yourself because for some people their hearts don't condemn them because they lie to themselves. But God looks for us to be truthful to Him and to ourselves. The thing to know is that God sees us, He knows us, He created us; therefore, it's just best to be honest. Another thing to know is that Satan knows you too, he is part of the reason that you lie to yourself. You must be honest to overcome Satan and all that he has to throw at you. God is there to protect you and to deliver you in His Son Jesus name but only if you're honest with Him and with yourself.

We must understand that Christianity is the way to the Living God of Israel, who is God to all of us, and to know that He has provided us a way through His Son Jesus Christ that we can escape eternal damnation and receive eternal Salvation is so much more than we could ever ask for. We must come to God with faith which is belief. Believing in Him and His Son and believing that through Jesus we receive the blessed Holy Spirit that leads us to eternal Salvation for our Souls.

To be a true servant of the Living God and His Son is a person that is honest before God. Whatever we are wrong in, we must with the mouth confess our sins before God in Jesus name and God will forgive us our sins because God is full of mercy and compassion, and will shower us with His love and His grace and His mercy. God is forever gentle and kind and just. He makes ways out of no ways, for us. God works miracles and blessings for His children and *Jesus* Christ is the advocate for our sins for salvation, and when we need Him most, He will be there for us at all times. God does not want any of us lost. For all of us belong to Him. Yet, He put a choice down in us and He allows us to choose between Heaven with Him or the Lake of Fire with Satan. It is up to us which way we go.

<<<<<<<   Faith of the Fifth Kingdom   >>>>>>>

We must believe that *Jesus* Christ is the Son of God and we must believe that God, His Father is God to the entire world. The God of Israel is also the God of the Gentiles. We must believe that God has made a way for the Gentiles to be engrafted into the fold of Israel that the whole world might be saved.

The one faith should be the same faith that is of the fifth kingdom, and that is to be a true Christian. The fifth kingdom is of Christ; God's Son was sent to us that the world through Him might be saved. Christ is soon to return to establish His kingdom.

Furthermore, we must go back to where *Jesus* started and follow his footsteps for the truth. We must truly fight for our souls to make it to Heaven by truly being a part of the fifth Kingdom that Daniel was talking about.

> **Daniel 2:44-45;** *And in the days of these kings shall the God of heaven set up a kingdom, which shall never be destroyed: and the*

kingdom shall not be left to other people, but it shall break in pieces and consume all these kingdoms, and it shall stand for ever. **45.** *Forasmuch as thou sawest that the stone was cut out of the mountain without hands, and that it brake in pieces the iron, the brass, the clay, the silver, and the gold; the great God hath made known to the king what shall come to pass hereafter: and the dream is certain, and the interpretation thereof sure.*

We must stop fighting among ourselves for self-righteousness and self-pride and look deep within ourselves for the truth. Search and seek the truth through the KJV Bible, through Encyclopedias, through history books and you will find that the answer is right there.

<<<<<<< Fifth Kingdom of today's society >>>>>>>

Love is the key. *Jesus* told us to be perfect as our Father which art in Heaven is perfect. The perfection that Jesus talks about is not that we as humans will never make a mistake but rather to have the perfect love. We are to love everybody as our Heavenly Father loves everyone. Love means I will tell you the truth, just the same way I want to hear the truth from you. The truth can be hard sometimes but it is needed in order to fight Satan. A wise man once told me; "know the truth and the truth shall set you FREE." We have Satan in this world to fight and he fights dirty; therefore, truth is our strength. God is truth. His word is truth, and, we, as His people should live in truth.

We must not conform to this world and its way of life. It is important to be in the world but not of the world. As God's children we are to live as Christians and be an example to those who don't know about God or His Son, *Jesus* Christ, our Messiah.

God is not that powerful voice that we see on Cecil B. DeMille's movie the Ten Commandments. God is a whisper. God is not forceful. God has given us the ability to make choices and He allows us to make our personal decisions to choose either Him or Satan. While on the other hand, Satan is forceful and tricky and plays dirty; therefore, it is up to us to seek out the truth. Because if we seek the truth with all our hearts, minds, bodies and souls we will find it out, for God does make it plain to see.

Another trick of Satan is to have you fight the truth by looking at relatives that have passed and gone and you will say to yourself, "I know this one or that one served the Lord, do you mean to tell me they were wrong?" You may also say, "I have been devoted for years, do you mean to tell me that I am wrong? Or that the loving pastor that taught me is wrong? Then who goes to Heaven and who goes to the Lake of Fire?" And my answer to it all would be, "each and every one of us have our own soul to worry about." It is enough to make sure your own soul gets to Heaven. So, if I bring you the truth so that you can escape the Lake of Fire, let everyone else take care of their selves.

I write to bring the truth to light and to show Satan's deceit because he is the father of lies and all that is evil. I am not writing to condemn but rather to set free. Any that have gone on before us whether Heaven will be their home or the Lake of Fire, is between God and them because to be perfectly honest with you, that is another trick of Satan. He has us putting people in Heaven or Hell and that is not ours to do. Also, in Heaven, there will be no more tears, no more crying only joy. It will not be as the song writers write it. Our bodies will be changed. We will not see mama or daddy or child, we will all be new. Which is a good thing because if we could recognize each other and don't see mama or daddy or child there, there will be tears in Heaven. But we will be as the Heavenly Angels, no more marrying, no recognizing family, and we will be all tongues, all nations, worshiping God, the Father, in the name of His Son *Jesus*, who is our Lord and Savior. There will be a new Heaven and a new Earth and this Earth will become the Lake of Fire with everlasting flames, heat and gnashing of teeth.

Moreover, it is so very important for every one of us to focus on our own souls. Because if we do this, then we can truly be of help to ourselves first than someone else. Making it to Heaven is the only time we can be selfish; naked you came into the world and naked shall you leave this world. As much as you love your Husband, Wife, Mama, Daddy, Sister, Brother, Daughter, Son, that special Aunt or Uncle, Grandmother, Grandfather, Nephew, Niece, Cousin, In-law, Family, or Friend, or whomever is special to you, everyone would have to go on his or her own. Soul Salvation is an individual thing. It is a decision that each individual makes. Does it mean to be so selfish that you don't help anybody else? Certainly not, because *Jesus* said, "thy shall love the Lord thy God with all thy heart, mind, body, and Soul and to love thy neighbor as thyself."

> **Mark 12:29-31** *And Jesus answered him, The first of all the commandments is, Hear, O Israel; The Lord Our God Is one Lord:* **30** *And thou shalt love the Lord thy God will all thy heart, and with all thy soul, and with all thy*

*mind, and with all thy strength: this is the first commandment. **31** And the second is like, namely this, thou shalt love thy neighbor as thyself. There is none other commandment greater than these.*

Also, in order to have this perfect love, you must love yourself first because if you love yourself enough to want to make it to Heaven when your time comes, you will do right by God, His Son, and everyone else. Also, an important note is that the above three verses cover the Ten Commandments because the first four Commandments are unto God and the last six Commandments are unto man, and as *Jesus* said, "there is none other Commandment greater than these," letting us know that *Jesus* did not do away with God's Ten Commandments; therefore, it is of utmost importance to keep the Ten Commandments of God. What Jesus did in Mark 12:29-31 was sum up the Ten Commandments. You must keep the Ten Commandments in order to be a part of the Fifth and final kingdom which is the Kingdom of our Christ.

Hitherto, we have television Evangelism and these Mega Churches, speaking philosophically, raising huge amounts of money, working miracles, prophesying, and teaching by way of books, CDs, and DVDs for prosperity only rather than soul salvation. And on Judgment Day, many will ask, "didn't we prophesy in thy name, didn't we cast out Devils in thy name, didn't we heal the sick in thy name?" And *Jesus* will say unto them, "depart from me, I know you not" because they didn't do the will of His Father, the Living God. There is so much healing, blessing and prosperity but no soul Salvation blessing, which is the most important. Souls for the Kingdom and not the things of this world because this world is only temporal, preparing us for the fifth and final Kingdom and our Eternal Glory.

<<<< Of the Fifth Kingdom--Where will you fit in? >>>>

We must be ready for the return of Christ. To be ready is to be like Christ. *Jesus* left us examples in the Bible of His self. He stayed in prayer with His Heavenly Father and He overcame all adversity. ***John 17:1;*** *These words spake Jesus, and lifted up his eyes to heaven and said, "Father, the hour is come; glorify thy Son, that thy Son also may glorify thee"…..****John 17:26;*** *And I have declared unto them thy name, and will declare it: that the love where with thou hast loved me may be in them, and I in them.* He showed us that the most important thing should be Heaven and the world to come, not this present world. This world is just a temporary place that we are traveling through until it is time for our Eternal home that will be Heaven or the Lake of Fire; it is our choice. That is the thing about the Living God; He lets us choose for ourselves. He shows us the way and gives us chance after chance after chance to get it right and walk the straight and narrow path that leads to Heaven even after we have made the wrong choice because He knows, that broad and easy is the way the leads to destruction, so He long-suffers because He wants everyone saved from sin. The choice is up to us to fight for our souls and all souls that want to be in Heaven in the end or to not fight and allow Satan to capture our soul for eternal damnation.

♦ *Where does the Catholic Church fit in?*

In reference to "broad is the way that leads to destruction," I must introduce a thought—even though there are certain rules that set us apart, yet these differences are rooted within the Catholic church for you may feel that Protestants and Catholics are different, when actually they are one and the same. So many protestant ways, stem from Catholicism which came from Constantine. That is why so many reference books that explain Christianity start with Catholicism instead of the true start of Christianity in Antioch among the disciples of Apostle Paul's time as described in **Acts 11:26;** *And when he had found him, he brought him unto Antioch. And it came to pass, that a whole year they assembled themselves with the church, and taught much people, and the disciples were called Christians first in Antioch.*

Furthermore, the Catholic Church claims Apostle Peter as their first Pope and this was because *Jesus* called Peter the rock on which the church is built; therefore, who claims Apostle Peter must be right. But that is the catch--

they claim Apostle Peter, the rock, but it was the first Christians which were the Jews and the Gentiles coming together as one, long before Constantine's time of the start of the Catholic Church. Catholic means universal, dubbing Christianity as their religion, when truly that claim belongs only to those who truly followed Christ whole heartedly. A true Christian is a servant of God, the Father through the Lord *Jesus* Christ being filled with the Holy Ghost with a strong faith of the promise of eternal life in Heaven by being Christ-like and being Over-comers in the end. A true Christian is neither Catholic nor Protestant but a true Christian is one that continues to follow Christ and His disciples, which included Apostle Paul, the one out of due season, before the Catholics came into power. Furthermore, Catholic faith does not follow the way of Jesus and His disciples, they've tried to change times and seasons as was spoken in **Daniel 7:25;** *And he shall speak great words against the most High, and shall wear out the saints of the most High, and think to change times and laws: and they shall be given into his hand until a time and times and the dividing of time.* As for the Protestants, the word 'Protestant' comes from protest, which they did against the Catholic Church. Even though they protested, many of the Catholic ways they kept and still keep many of the Catholic ways to this day and include them in their dogma.

Furthermore, instead of any Catholics or Protestants being mad with me for the truth that I state they should be mad with Constantine who had devious motives when conforming Christianity to Roman ways. Had he been a true convert he wouldn't have changed any ways but rather just joined in and followed Christianity whole heartedly. But instead he deceived his own followers and helped Satan to deceive the world who follow any of the Roman Catholic ways. The truth is the truth and it's just that simple.

♦ *Trinity as apposed to Godhead*

Another key point, think deeply within your own mind, heart, and soul, and ask yourself, does it make sense to have so many different faiths within one religion? And, if there is truly one God and He only has one Son, and only one Holy Ghost power which was sent to comfort us all, then why all the different ways to the ONE? There should only be one way. Furthermore, if trinity is right, then wouldn't we need to get filled with the Holy Ghost three times instead of once? You would need to get a spirit from the father, a spirit from the son, and a spirit from the Holy Ghost. But rather, *Jesus* said He will send us a comforter. **John 14:16;** *And I will pray to the Father, and He shall give you another Comforter, that he may abide with you forever.* This comforter is the Holy Ghost, which is one Spirit, from the one God, which is the Godhead spoken of in **Colossians 2:9;** *For in him dwelleth all the fullness of the Godhead bodily.* Besides, the way of trinity stems from the Catholic Church and it is different from the truth.

◆ Ten Commandments vs. Ceremonial Law

Apostle Paul taught throughout the New Testament to be watchful of this transformation. For instance, it is fine to have different leaders because Apostle Paul, himself, was fine with that; however, the catch is that each leader may have different ways of teaching but each leader should be teaching the same truth. If one teaches to believe in the law and another teaches there is no need for the law, aren't they teaching totally different things? Apostle Paul taught the churches how to stay uniformed and not to drift off into uncertainty. As the Bible shows Apostle Paul was to lead the Gentiles (anyone that is not a Jew) and Apostle Peter was to lead Israel. ***Galatians 2:7;*** *But contrariwise, when they saw that the gospel of the uncircumcision was committed unto me, as the gospel of the circumcision was unto Peter.* Apostle Paul and Apostle Peter taught the same truths, just to different groups of people. There are many people that disagree with me. They say that Apostle Paul teaches contrary to Christ, even though Christ is the one that appointed him, also, Apostle Peter, who *Jesus* said is the Rock of the new way, spoke for Apostle Paul in *II Peter 3:15-17*.

In addition, it is important to note that when Apostle Paul speaks of nailing the handwritten ordinances to the cross, he is speaking of the Ceremonial Laws and not the Ten Commandment Laws.

> *Colossians 2:13-14 And you, being dead in your sins and the uncircumcision of your flesh, hath he quickened together with him, having forgiven you all trespasses; **14** Blotting out the handwriting of ordinances that was against us, which was contrary to us, and took it out of the way, nailing it to his cross;*

Throughout the New Testament when Apostle Paul speaks of doing away with the Law, he is speaking of the Ceremonial Laws only, not the Ten Commandment Laws. Who can better explain doing away with the Ceremonial Laws, then Apostle Paul who once was a Pharisee and was raised up studying the laws? He knew it inside-out, as a matter of fact, before he was converted, he persecuted the church because of the Ceremonial Laws. And *Jesus* showed him that he was not doing the will of God but to follow the way of *Jesus* without the Ceremonial Laws is the new way.

Furthermore, Jesus, Himself, says that He did not come to destroy the law but to fulfill the law, meaning the Ten Commandment Laws. *Jesus* was the sacrificial Lamb to replace the Ceremonial Laws which were not able to save the people.

> **Romans 8:3;** *For what the law could not do, in that it was weak through the flesh, God sending his own Son in the likeness of sinful flesh, and for sin, condemned sin in the flesh:*

The Ceremonial Laws were written by Moses as instructed by God, for the people; but, the Ten Commandment Laws were written by the finger of God which stood apart from the Ceremonial Laws. **Exodus 31:18;** *And he gave unto Moses, when he had made an end of communing with him upon mount Sinai, two tables of testimony, tables of stone, written with the finger of God.*

Christ was fulfilling the Law of the Ten Commandments; therefore, when Christ showed the Pharisees things that could be done on the Sabbath day, he was not doing away with the Sabbath day, but rather he was instituting it and expounding on what the Sabbath was truly about, and He would know because He was Lord of the Sabbath.

> ***Matthew 12:8;*** *For the Son of man is Lord even of the sabbath day.* ***Mark 2:28;*** *Therefore, the Son of man is Lord also of the sabbath.* ***Luke 6:5;*** *And he said unto them, that the Son of man is Lord also of the sabbath.*

Thus, the seventh day Sabbath of the Ten Commandments should be kept. Not the first day Sunday, because Jesus never instituted keeping the first day, Sunday; neither, did any of his Apostles not even the one out of season, which was Apostle Paul. All the Apostles of *Jesus* were Sabbath keepers which falls back to the Ten Commandments that were written by God.

> ***Exodus 24:12;*** *And the Lord said unto Moses, Come up to me into the mount, and be there:*

and I will give thee tables of stone, and a law, and commandments which I have written; that thou mayest teach them. **Exodus 34:1;** *And the Lord said unto Moses, Hew thee two tables of stone like unto the first: and I will write upon these tables the words that were in the first tables, which thou brakest.*

If we no longer have to keep the seventh day Sabbath which is from Friday eve to Saturday eve then we can kill, we can steal but the laws all over the world says no to these and four other commandments it's just that no one wants to honor and obey the Living God because the first four commandments are to the Living God and the last six of the Ten Commandments are to man; therefore, so many Christian and most non-Christian alike agree on six commandments as a matter of fact you break the law of the lands when you break the last six commandments but we must understand the trick of Satan because the first four commandments are unto the Living God—Satan wants you to break those laws knowing that when you break the first four you will automatically not keep the rest either. The only way that a person gets to go to Heaven without keeping the Ten Commandments is if they never were shown the truth but that is not a chance that I would be willing to take if I were you. It truly isn't something that I would play with. People look at the sinner that was on the cross that asked *Jesus* for forgiveness and *Jesus* told him he would be with Him in Paradise and that was because the Living God is fair the man requested forgiveness on time. But you may die instantly without a chance to ask for forgiveness.

Furthermore, if you're reading this book and still feel that the Ten Commandments belong to the Jews and are no longer necessary. You should read **Revelation 22: 14-16 14.** Blessed are they that do His commandments, that they may have right to the tree of life, and may enter in through the gates into the city. **15.** For without are dogs, and sorcerers, and whoremongers, and murderers, and idolaters, and whosoever loveth and maketh a lie. **16.** I *Jesus* have sent mine Angel to testify unto you these things in the churches. I am the root and offspring of David, and the bright and morning star.

♦ Melchizedek Priesthood

Moreover, that is why the veil of the temple rent in twain, because *Jesus* replaced the Ceremonial Laws. **Mark 15:37-39;** *And Jesus cried with a loud voice, and gave up the ghost.* ***38.*** *And the veil of the temple was rent in twain from the top to the bottom.* ***39.*** *And when the centurion, which stood over against him, saw that he so cried out, and gave up the ghost, he said, truly this man was the Son of God.* Also, the Levitical priesthood was done away with because Christ was a priest after the order of Melchizedek.

> **Hebrews 7:11-17;** *If therefore perfection were by the Levitical priesthood, (for under it the people received the law,) what further need was there that another priest should rise after the order of Melchizedek, and not be called after the order of Aaron?* ***12.*** *For the priesthood being changed, there is made of necessity a change also of the law.* ***13.*** *For he of whom these things are spoken pertaineth to another tribe, of which no man gave*

attendance at the altar. **14.** *For it is evident that our Lord sprang out of Judah; of which tribe Moses spake nothing concerning priesthood.* **15.** *And it is yet far more evident: for that after the similitude of Melchizedek there ariseth another priest,* **16.** *Who is made, not after the law of a carnal commandment, but after the power of an endless life.* **17.** *For he testifieth, Thou art a priest for ever after the order of Melchizedek.*

Melchizedek was God in the flesh whom Abraham gave his tithes to. **Hebrews 6:1-3;** *For this Melchizedek, king of Salem, priest of the most high God, who met Abraham returning from the slaughter of the kings, and blessed him;* **2.** *To whom also Abraham gave a tenth part of all; first being by interpretation King of righteousness, and after that also King of Salem, which is, King of peace;* **3.** *Without father, without mother, without descent, having neither beginning of days, nor end of life; but made like unto the Son of God; abideth a priest continually.*

♦ *Muslims*

In the meantime, America looks at Muslims as the real threat of mankind as the one spoken of in Apocalypse. When truly we should fear what makes us reprobates and not true Christians, and it is not the Muslims. The Muslim Nation is of Ishmael's descendants, who is brother to Israel, Isaac's descendants, and both are of the blood of Abraham. Yet, it is important to know that Isaac was the chosen child, he was the promise child. All the world has a chance to be saved through Isaac's descendants. Ishmael's descendants must come to the knowledge of the truth before it will be too late for them. To sum up, Ishmael's descendants have been worshipping a false God that they learned from a false prophet, because they like the Jews should be worshipping Christ and in that they would be worshipping the Living God of Israel which is all of our God. Further, they fight and kill their chosen brother. In addition, I want to bring some points to you that make what I say clear to you and it is as follows:

a) God is not the author of confusion as shown in the KJV Bible--*I Corinthians 14:33; For God is not the author of confusion, but of peace, as in all churches of the saints.*

b) God would not have shown Daniel twice from the Angel Gabriel His Son's kingdom to come as the KJV Bible shows—*Daniel 8:16; And I heard a man's voice between the banks of Ulai, which called, and said, Gabriel, make this man to understand the vision* and *Daniel 9:21; Yea, which I was speaking in prayer, even the man Gabriel, whom I had seen in the vision at the beginning, being caused to fly swiftly, touched me about the time of the evening oblation.* The prophet Daniel shows us the four beasts and five kingdoms, which are Nebuchadnezzar, King of Babylon, first beast and first kingdom, Darius and Cyrus Kings of Medes and Persia, the second beast and second kingdom, Alexander the Great, king of Greece, the third beast and third kingdom, and

Rome the fourth beast and fourth kingdom, then Jesus Christ, the fifth and final Kingdom. If Ishmael and his descendants were to lead as a kingdom, Daniel would have shown this but rather, Daniel shows that Christ and His Kingdom will be the fifth and final Kingdom which is of God and Abraham's descendants both natural and spiritual.

c) Furthermore, God would not send the Angel Gabriel to Zechariah and to Mary as shown in the KJV Bible—***Luke 1:18-19;*** *And Zechariah said unto the angel, whereby shall I know this? For I am an old man, and my wife well stricken in years **19.** And the Angel answering said unto him I am Gabriel, that stand in the presence of God; and am sent to speak unto thee, and to show thee these glad tidings.* Six months later Gabriel appeared to Mary ***Luke 1:26 -28;*** *And in the sixth month the angel Gabriel was sent from God unto a city of Galilee named Nazareth. **27.** To a virgin* *espoused to a man whose name was Joseph of the house of David; and the virgin's name was Mary* ***28.*** *And the angel came in unto her, and said, Hail, thou that art highly favored, the Lord is with thee: blessed art thou among women* **Luke 1:31-35;** *And, behold, thou shalt conceive in thy womb, and bring forth a son, and shalt call his name JESUS* ***32.*** *He shall be great, and shall be called the Son of the Highest: and the Lord God shall give unto him the throne of his father David:* ***33.*** *And he shall reign over the house of Jacob forever; and of his Kingdom there shall be no end.* ***34.*** *Then said Mary unto the angel, How shall this be, seeing I know not a man?* ***35.*** *And the angel answered and said unto her, The Holy Ghost shall come upon thee, and the power of the Highest shall over-shadow thee: therefore, also that holy thing which shall be born of thee shall be called the Son of God.*

Now, I say again, God is not the author of confusion; Gabriel appeared to Daniel the prophet of the Old

Testament letting us know of Jesus to come and His Kingdom. Then Gabriel appeared to Zechariah because his son was going to be John the Baptist who was to be the forerunner of *Jesus* who prepared the way for *Jesus* when he came. Then Gabriel appeared last to Mary to let her know that she shall have a son from the Living God and His name shall be Jesus. To clarify further would it even make sense for the Living God to send the Angel Gabriel to prepare for His Son and show that His Son shall be the fifth and final Kingdom and then send Gabriel to Muhammad for Ishmael's descendants to tell Muhammad to announce God as Allah and to announce *Jesus* as being one of the prophets? Even the Quran shows that Jesus is special: Quran 3:43-44 and 3:46-48. Further, to instruct Ishmael's descendants to hate and kill Israel His chosen? Even Ishmael did not hate his brother because he joined his brother Isaac to bury their father Abraham.

Most importantly anyone that does not acknowledge that *Jesus* Christ as the Son of God and our Savior is the Antichrist. The Muslim Nation is brother to Israel and blood of Abraham and what shall become of them is in the Living God's hands. For they worship a false god from a false prophet and fight against their chosen brother. God will judge between them and Israel. It is a fight that does not belong to America. America did not become a target until we started supplying weapons to Islamic countries and getting involved where we should not have been involved. Then when our shrewd involvement caused retaliation we go to war. Am I saying that Al Qaeda was justified? No, Al Qaeda was wrong; however, I am saying that America's predisposition was not right either. Does America choose Israel because Israel is the chosen nation of God and because it is the right thing to do? Or, does America choose Israel because they hate Israel's brother? Oh, what a hypocritical stand on America's part. God looks at the whole thing and He will judge

America at the end along with everyone else that has not, nor does not truly stand with Israel. Speaking of Judgement of America, the next page will go into Blood Stained America.

♦ Blood Stained America

Consequently, America is a blood-stained land because it has the blood of the Native Americans and African Americans and the slavery of all Blacks on their hands; however, it did give freedom of religion and a way for the church, the one true church of God to be saved and spread abroad, all throughout the world. I am not speaking of different forms of religion, nor the different ways to Christianity; but rather I'm speaking about true Christianity that *Jesus* ordained through all of His twelve Apostles and with Apostle Paul being the last true Apostle. The knowledge of *Jesus* Christ is published throughout the world from America, which establish freedom of religion.

Therefore, even though there was so much wrong that was done in America when it comes to the death of the Native Americans and the taking away of their land from them while killing and brutalizing and enslaving Blacks to build a land that was stolen. Two good things came out of it all and they were the freedom of religion and the freedom of speech.

It's also important to state that it was God's plan for America to be the place where truth would come from. But it's just as important if not more important to know that it was not His plan to Kill and take the Native Americans land away from them nor was it His plan to enslave Blacks nor brutalize nor kill them in order to build America. God's truth could have still spread just as it did if not even faster through love and cooperation with those who were already here, which included Blacks, because not all Blacks came from Africa but where already here. All Blacks were not brought from Africa as we've been taught but were from America when they founded this country. The freedom of religion and the freedom of speech were of God but everything else was not.

♦ Homosexuality

Also, we must look closely at America, for America has deeply fallen and become as Sodom and Gomorrah, wanting Christians to justify homosexuality when it is against God. You may look at what I say and feel that America is supposed to be the land of the free, which gave us freedom of speech and freedom of religion. Then why is it wrong to be homosexual? Shouldn't a homosexual have freedom of sex? To that I say, I am not trying to take away anyone's freedom, and truly that is what I am stressing that a Christian should have the freedom to speak against anything that is not of God which happens to be homosexuality among other sins. Do I feel that we should go all over America announcing it as loud as we can? No, I feel that it should be an in-house thing; in other words, within the church realm. What people do before coming to God is up to them; however, once in God you become a new creature for all things become new.

> ***Genesis 19:1;*** *And there came two angels to Sodom at even; and Lot sat in the gate of*

Sodom: and Lot seeing them rose up to meet them; and he bowed himself with his face toward the ground: **Genesis 19: 13;** *For we will destroy this place, because the cry of them is waxen great before the face of the Lord; and the Lord hath sent us to destroy it.* **Genesis 19: 24-25;** *Then the Lord rained upon Sodom and upon Gomorrah brimstone and fire from the Lord out of heaven;* **25.** *And he overthrew those cities, and all the plain, and all the inhabitants of the cities, and that which grew upon the ground.*

Jude 7; *Even as Sodom and Gomorrah, and the cities about them in like manner, giving themselves over to fornication, and going after strange flesh, are set forth for an example, suffering the vengeance of eternal fire.*

Just as important, so many Christians are too afraid to stand up and speak out, fearing that they shall be judged as discriminating. It is the trick of Satan to make a Christian feel that they are not loving everyone if they speak against wrong, which is not true. One can speak against wrong and most definitely love because true love is to save a soul from sin. Wrong is wrong, not just homosexuality but that little white lie is just as wrong. Sin is sin and all it will do is take a soul to the Lake of Fire. Can I say that homosexuality is wrong and love a homosexual? The answer is yes. To be perfect in God is to have the perfect love and that is to love everyone. Do I agree with violence against homosexuals? Most definitely not. Do I say we should make a homosexual feel lower than life? No, of course not. I will never forget my experience with an individual that was gay, that person showed me love and compassion when no one else did. So, it is not for a Christian to put anybody down or to act as if the sin of a homosexual is the only sin. However, as a true Christian we should not condone homosexuality. And as for same sex marriage, it is against God; therefore, no true church of God should perform the marriage nor be forced to do so. People look for signs of the end time and the signs have already come and gone, as King Solomon said, what is future has been already. ***Ecclesiastes 3:15*** *That which hath been is now; and that which is to be hath already been: and God requireth that which is past.* America needs to follow Christ before it is too late, all the Prophets of the Old Testament and the Apostles and Prophets of the New Testament lead us to Christ.

I must also add that the Christian should stand on the truth and not be swayed from it, yet not leaving off love and compassion which must be shown, also showing there is an alternative to sin and at the same time, showing there is a better way. I was looking at this lesbian couple and I could tell that they really loved each other and didn't have much but each other. And in seeing them, I realized that some people don't start out as homosexuals but rather due to rejections and loneliness in life, and this one person comes along and love them for who they are, then he/she becomes someone that cares about them and for them, and now the church says that the only one that loves them and sticks by them is evil for them. Also, there are cases when boys and girls have been molested by their own gender and it just became a way of life, and they already have all this past pain in their lives, and the church adds to their pain that they are living in sin. Further, you have women and men that say they had the feelings for their own gender ever since they could remember from a child. And these are just some situations that the Gay and Lesbian Community face, yet each and every one of these situations can be addressed. And that is through one word and it is LOVE. For love covers a multitude of sins. A Christian should be able to invite a Gay or Lesbian individual or couple to church, accept them for who they are and leave the rest into God's hands. I can be a Christian and have Gay and Lesbian friends because I know how to tell them the truth and where I stand and at the same time, respect who they are and not work on changing them but leave it in God's hands. My advice to the Gay and Lesbian friends that I have had has always been, be who you are until God takes it away and it is just that simple. When coming to church, it should be a happy place, a place where nobody is judged, a place of unconditional love, and a place of acceptance. Will the word come from the Pulpit on how and why homosexuality is wrong? Yes, but so will the word about lying, about hate, about anything that hinders any of us from going to Heaven. Should the word be coming across the Pulpit about homosexuality as the main topic because of a homosexual member? No, most definitely not because it is not the only sin. Should members be voicing their opinions? No. That is the problem with so many Churches; the members don't stay in their place, and leave things up to their leader. The point is not to beat a person down. But just as God has long suffered with us until we gave up our vices, some still haven't, is the way we are to be for everyone.

♦ Hitler and Jews

Another thing, America has been on borrowed time because it truly is a blood-stained land. America was taken from the Native Americans, who can never get their land back. America became wealthy through the blood and sweat of African-American Slaves. And the world looks at Hitler and what he did to the Jews. When the Native Americans and the African-Americans, which truly are one in the same, have it far worse than the Jews with Hitler and if anyone thinks that is not so, let me paint a picture for you; Imagine Hitler never being taken out of power and died and left his children in charge. Then imagine generation after generation passed with his children still being in charge.

Next, imagine the Jews fighting for equal rights and then you have some of Hitler's children that say we are looking bad to the world, it is wrong, give them some rights, and most of Hitler's children decide to give the Jews some rights. They even elect a Chancellor that is half German and half Jew. And Hitler's children tell the world, see we most definitely are fair now, we are just, and we are good. But at the same time, in most of the political high positions, Hitler's children are in charge and throughout the country, Laws are passed to not let the Jews grow but so far, BEATINGS and KILLINGS still take place among the Jews, just in different ways and this goes on at the same time that Jews start killing Jews, which is a happy form of genocide for Hitler's children while at the same time saying to the world, with their actions, see why we treat the Jews the way we treat them.

Now, let's imagine that one of Hitler's children go too far with poor treatment of the Jews, where the world that is looking says we thought you all were better. So, Hitler's other children make an example of that one sibling to show that the Jews are being treated fairly; yet, the example is not too harsh a punishment and at the same time, Hitler's children tighten up on the laws making things worse for the Jews. And everybody else in Germany prospers except for the majority of the Jews, and oppression still is a way of life for a Jew, and there is no way out for a Jew except to live life and die. Now, let's change names, for instance Hitler's name changes to our forefathers like George Washington, a slave owner and so many others, that's what makes much of white America worse than Hitler because at least the Jews have a person. With America it's the Government and its constituents so who do we blame? But remain under constraints. Now, let's proceed and change the name of Hitler's children to White America, and change the name of the Jews to Native Americans and African-Americans. Do I show this to say that all White America is no good? No, most definitely not. Neither do I show this to show blame or to encourage hatred. As Christians, we are to love everyone in spite of any circumstances. And truthfully speaking, if it were not for the White Americans that did stand for truth and justice, there would be absolutely no truth and justice for any minority in America.

Furthermore, it must be said that Black on Black crime is rampant and the same with the Native Americas and those things are on us, not on the White man, and this is also the truth. Furthermore, even during the time of slavery there were some White Americans that didn't own slaves and wanted no part of it. Also, there were so many White

Americans that died fighting for the cause of the minority, such as John Brown his family who devoted themselves and gave their lives to set slaves free. Yet, I write this to show the truth about what is truly going on in this Country. It has not been so long ago that the Klu Klux Klan were hanging our black men and killing black women and children, and now they have gotten away with the violence so long that they have embedded themselves into our Legislative system, our police fraternities, in all hierarchy that blacks look for to uphold us as American Citizens. In addition, blacks have their own kind putting them down and justifying unjustifiable deaths just to gain power such as Candace Owens, who says that racially motivated police brutality is a myth—I haven't heard about her until I seen her on YouTube and the things she said hurt me deeply to the heart, it was so bad that it took God to bring me out of the deep hurt that I felt. I am the first to say that there are white policemen that are good and that do their job well by looking out for everyone equally and treating everyone right equally. But at the same time there are many white policemen that brutalize and harass the black race, especially our males.

To give everyone a clear picture as to how bad it is for blacks especially our males but our females as well—white policemen know that they are being recorded and don't stop the unnecessary killing.

Also, what makes it worse the courts set them free, if they ever get tried. And another thing if a white policeman kills a black man wrongfully in Maryland he'll go to Virginia and get his job back. In this I'm just naming two states but if you look into the history of the white policemen that have been killing and when the public speaks out and they lose their job in that state check to see if they have a job as a police officer in another state. What white America don't know is that this is not new it's been going on for years. We never had any rights when it came to justice. We, as the black race, are looked at as guilty first and must prove our innocence when it's supposed to be the other way around.

Then Candace Owens and blacks like minded feel in order to be a Republican you have to tear down your own race but there is a strong preacher who is also on YouTube who had me looking at President Trump in another light and his name is Marcus Rogers and blacks as well as whites, who are Democrat, need to hear what things he has to say, especially if you are a Christian. Marcus Rogers shows how and why we should re-elect President Trump and he does it without tearing down blacks. This book is not telling anybody which way to vote but it's important to look at all sides and weigh what is best for this country. People will look at this and say Trump is a liar, he keeps the country divided and I say to that the Democrats take God out of the equation and the Republicans take Humanity out of the equation. Both sides are equally wrong for different reasons.

I'm neither Republican nor Democrat, I've always voted for the lesser of two evils which happened to be the Democrats most of the time but this time I have to go deep because both sides are equal in being evil but I'm not looking at the Republicans as a party because I'm totally against most of what they stand for as a party but I'm only looking at President Trump, the leader and the commander whose ideas don't totally agree with the party anyway and what he is doing and what he plans to do that line-up with

God. For one he's strong on being with Israel, God's chosen, and the Democrats are not and he wants to keep God in everything that the Democrats want to take God out of.

It's not white Evangelical Christians that should be asking strong questions about who will be taking us where biblically all Christians should be asking these questions.

Then, there are those who say that President Trump is dividing the country when this country has always been divided. It was divided when former President Obama was in the White House and he said everything right. Here we are still fighting the same fight that Dr. Martin Luther King, Jr. and Malcolm X fought during their time. There are those who think because we have so many interracial couples that prejudice is over in America, I tell you to look at one man for your answer and that is the former President of the United States of America, Barack Hussein Obama.

In my lifetime, I had never seen a president treated with such disrespect among his own peers as I have seen with President Obama until President Trump but that's another story for another reason, something that should be looked at through Marcus Rogers eyes. I think it should be said that I don't know Marcus Rogers and I've never corresponded with him. I just seen him on YouTube and thought he had a lot of truth.

Now back to what to look at when you feel that prejudice is over in America. Importantly, why was the former President known as the first black President? Why was or is not known as America's first true President because he is both white and black; therefore, he should have been representing all that is possible in America as the great melting pot? But white America is still the same, if you have any black in you, no matter if you are part white, you are still considered a slave and no more. I show this to show the truth.

Furthermore, God has seen enough bloodshed and enough injustice in America for America not to be serving the true and Living God and His Son, *Jesus* Christ our Messiah earnestly, which would be a grave mistake. The only thing that has been keeping America thus far has been the freedom of religion and speech because despite all the false religions, the truth has gotten out and spread throughout the world. The truth that the Living God of Israel is all our God and He has a Son who is *Jesus* Christ our Messiah that left us with a Comforter, the blessed Holy Ghost, which there is one Lord, one Faith, and one Baptism, and the Father of us all, and this is right and true and the means by which the Godhead meaning has been attained, yet, when ignored that is where the problem lies within Society.

♦ Men vs. Women's place in the Lord

Another important thing is that the women in this country have gone too far. There are Women Apostles, Women Bishops, just a Woman Preacher, period, is wrong. So many women are not in their place in America nor in the much of the Christian world.

Satan is tricky, we look else-where in the world were women are treated less than human—as in genital mutilation which is a horrible travesty when a woman's private parts are all cut out and then sewed up with only enough opening to release body fluids and then upon her wedding night her groom takes a knife and cut her open then forces himself in her and if they survive this unholy degradation, there is something known as "honor killing," when if a woman is raped, she can be killed by a family member for not remaining a virgin, or if a family member believes she has been sleeping with a man, no proof, just a thought, she can be killed by a family member as an "honor killing," even after an autopsy shows her to have been a virgin, there is no repentance of the "honor killing," which in itself is beyond being deplorable. There can even be an "honor killing" if she marries somebody she loves as opposed to a pre-arranged marriage, and we, Americans look at this and say that is not right, and that is so very true; it is not right and really it is so wrong that there are no words to truly describe just how wrong it is, because those countries and some men within our own country take the submit part and leave off the treat-her-right part, to love her as you love your soul.

Yet, God will judge them and their outcome is in God's hands. Yet at the same time, neither should women be treated as equal to men and especially not above a man, because both incidents are equally wrong. And if a woman reads this and gets mad because she finds herself out of place, do not get mad with me because I am just speaking the truth. Do not fault man or God. If you want to blame anyone, blame Eve because in the Garden of Eden, man and woman were one but when Eve let the serpent entice her, the punishment on women was to be subject unto the man and experience hard labor when bearing children, and to the men, hard labor and sweat—when working, and death on all of us.

> ***Genesis 3:16-19;*** *Unto the woman he said, I will greatly multiply thy sorrow and thy conception: in sorrow thou shalt bring forth children: and thy desire shall be to thy husband, and he shall rule over thee.* ***17.*** *And unto Adam he said Because thou hast hearkened unto the voice of thy wife, and hast eaten of the tree, of which I commanded thee, saying, Thou shalt not eat of it: cursed is the ground for thy sake; in sorrow shalt thou eat of it all the days of thy life;* ***18.*** *Thorns also and thistles shall it bring forth to thee; and thou shalt eat the herb of the field:* ***19.*** *In the sweat of thy face shalt thou eat bread, till thou return unto the ground; for out of it wast thou taken: for dust thou art, and unto dust shalt thou return.*

Importantly, the men have a duty to love their wives. ***Ephesians 5: 22-25;*** *Wives, submit yourselves unto your own husbands, as unto the Lord.* ***23.*** *For the husband is* *the head of the wife, even as Christ is the head of the church: and he is the savior of the body.* **24.** *Therefore as the church is subject unto Christ, so let the wives be to their own husbands in everything.* **25.** *Husbands, love your wives, even as Christ also loved the church, and gave himself for it;* **Ephesians 5:28;** *So, ought men to love their wives as their own bodies. He that loveth his wife, loveth himself.*

In addition, the things people do in the name of God— is it the true Living God or have they been deceived? *Jesus* said there will be those that will kill you and think they do God's will. As so many Muslims that kill Christians and anyone who does not have the Muslim belief. Furthermore, Many of the early Christians were killed by Jews, as well as the Romans and even after Constantine, many were killed that did not conform to what Rome instituted as the new way of Christianity. And the past has a way of repeating itself, if we don't learn from it. Due to the way things are going in the United States Court System, it will soon be a crime of discrimination for a Christian to say that homosexuality is wrong; and it will also be a form of discrimination to not marry homosexual couples. The very act could give a Christian jail time. Sounds to me like Apostle Paul's time all over again when Christians were persecuted for speaking the truth. All this shows us that Jesus shall return soon to gather His own; therefore, anyone wanting to make it to Heaven need to consider what things are being said and truly examine what is being said from the heart, mind, and soul.

◆ Existence of Angels

Importantly, Satan knows that the only way to Heaven is to be a true Christian and we should not get too deep into the existence of Angels, but there are Fallen Angels which shine as Angels of Light but are not righteous, then there are the Living God's Holy Angels that are righteous and for this book I will not go to deep into it but at least bring things to, you the reader's attention. For example, trying to find out names other than what is in the Bible, because if we go too far with Angels, we begin to worship them and that is why Angels are not emphasized about in the Bible. To know that Heavenly Angels fight for us and watch over us is good enough. We must also keep in mind that there are fallen Angels which can appear and deceive many to turn away from following our Heavenly Father and our Lord and Savior, *Jesus* Christ. To be honest with you, if you keep the Ten Commandments, you will know that it is a sin to make any image of anything in Heaven above or in the earth beneath. Therefore, the Sistine Chapel, no matter how beautiful it is, it is not of

God. Any picture of *Jesus* is not of God, because He was both human and divine. As strong as this sound, the cross should not be made. There also should not be any pictures drawn of Satan and his fallen Angels. Some people took it too far by saying no drawing at all, and that is not true. We can draw the Apostles, or anything pertaining to life here on Earth. We can draw the Universe. We can draw the imaginations of our minds. We have a lot of freedom to create art, in paintings, drawings, carvings, and such. But there is a boundary and the boundary is set for a reason. And that reason is if God says no, then it is no. Just like in the Garden of Eden, God told them to eat of every tree except one and on the day, you eat of it, you shall surely die. Adam and Eve ate of it and didn't die instantly but lost instant connection with God; therefore, dying instantly spiritually and eventually dying natural, and brought spiritual and natural death upon all of us. And *Jesus*, the second Adam brought life back to us, with a return to spiritual connection with God the Father and naturally life, to not fear the grave because we shall live again in Heaven for all eternity if we obey the will of God, our Heavenly Father.

♦ Search for the Truth

Above all, we must search the truth out for ourselves. We must thoroughly examine what is presented to not justify ourselves because God is the only one that does the justification. But rather, we should fight for our Souls to be in Heaven in the end, and to know that we are forever learning but should come to the knowledge of truth. Furthermore, I have studied the Quran for the same length of time as I have studied the Bible before I believed and also, I prayed every time that I read the Quran just as I pray every time before I read the Bible. In my search for the truth, I have studied many religions and I found the truth in the KJV Bible and in *Jesus* Christ, my Messiah when God took a wretch like me and forgave me of all my numerous sins. He filled me with the precious gift of the Holy Ghost when I gave up everything in this world and laid out before Him with my whole Body, Mind, and Soul, while calling on the name of *Jesus* then in came the Holy Ghost and I was taken up to Heaven and I heard myself speaking which is my testimony showing you that

God is still in the saving business. I'm speaking just to you, the one who feels that you are too bad of a person to be saved or to you, the one that feels you don't know about God so where do you start? How? What? Why? Are questions that come to your mind or to you, the one that is just plain tired of the pains of this world. Well, I want you, and you, and you, and YOU, who thinks He doesn't see you, to know that God forgives all sins and He loves the repenting heart that is before Him asking for forgiveness for sins and do know that *Jesus* died for all of us all our sins, to be able to overcome this world and make it to the next one. Do know that this book is the beginning of a way to eternal joy and peace with no more tears. We should thank God when truth is presented to us, listen and obey from the heart to be acceptable by our Heavenly Father and His Son, our Lord and Savior, *Jesus* Christ. You should know from the heart that this world is temporary and everything in it. It's just our training ground, and our means to our eternal home. Whether it will be everlasting peace and joy with no more suffering, no more pains of this life but to be in Heaven with God the Father and *Jesus* Christ, the Son, the blessed Holy Ghost and the Host of Heavenly Angels; or everlasting torment where there will be an unquenchable fire and gnashing of teeth and suffering throughout eternity, with no hope, no joy, no peace, along with Satan, who deceived you and his fallen Angels. The choice is yours. God has given us the power to make choices. We either honestly look at what has been given to us, weigh the matter truthfully and make a decision whether we go left or right. **Matthew 6:24;** *No man can serve two masters: for either he will hate the one and love the other; or else he will hold to the one, and despise the other. Ye cannot serve God and mammon.*

◆ *Follow Tradition or Truth*

Finally, the problem with us as a people is that we question God with questions that we already have the answers to, for the answers lie within us. Should we follow tradition or should we follow our Heavenly Father and His Son, Jesus? Should we follow the majority?

> ***Matthew 7:13-14;*** *Enter ye in at the strait gate: for wide is the gate, and broad is the way, that leadeth to destruction, and many there be which go in thereat.* ***14.*** *Because strait is the gate, and narrow is the way, which leadeth unto life, and few there be that find it.*

The choice is up to us because God has placed in each of us the answer to these questions. We must go back to the true beginning of Christianity to find Heaven. As God had revealed to me long ago, if someone asks you, "where is your church?" Say that it was before time began! And if they ask you, "what is your faith and your denomination?" Say to them that it is the Living God and

His Son, Jesus Christ my Messiah! Does it mean that we should not assemble ourselves together? No. Does it mean that we should not have a church? No. But it does mean that we have to have the true understanding of what Church is all about and what the assembling of ourselves together, truly mean. We must go back to the basics and stand our ground for the truth. We must stand as one unit and fight Satan on every side through the blood of Jesus. We must always want the truth, no matter how much it hurts, because the truth sometimes can be extremely painful but at the end, it yields peaceable fruit. We must be the seed that fall into the good ground as Jesus has said in a parable. We must spread the truth, all of the truth. We must live and die and live again for the truth, for ourselves first than to be a help to anyone that wants to be in Heaven in the end. Do know, if you have read this book, that God loves you and He wants you to know the truth for the truth shall set you free. He sent His Son *Jesus* Christ our Messiah our King that we could be free of sin and that death would have no more hold on us and that Heaven can be all our homes in the end. For all nations and all tongues shall be in Heaven. For the Jews and the Gentiles shall be one.

ISRAEL'S *GOD* IS *GOD* AND HE HAS A SON, *JESUS CHRIST* OUR *MESSIAH*, WHO SHALL RETURN FOR US WHO ARE HIS.

About the Author

I am a mother and grandmother, daughter, sister, and aunt who loves my family well and I spread this same truth to those who know me. I am a Christian that have been in the Lord for thirty-nine years and have stumbled and backed-up along the way but mostly fought and stood and continue to stand for the truth in the Lord. It's been hard and a long fight but worth it every step of the way because God in *Jesus*' name has been with me and continues to be with me every step of the way through the blessed Holy Ghost which has led me into all truth and continues to lead and guide me. Also, I am a poet, who loves to write, draw, and paint. I am a college graduate with two Associate degrees, one degree in Art and the other degree in Business Management and I am working on my Bachelor's degree with my major in Business Administration and my minor in Entrepreneurship: Small Business. I plan on graduating with my Bachelor's degree in Fall 2021.

If there are any questions or comments, feel free to contact me and I will try and respond personally to each one of you:

Andrea Chambers
P.O. Box 6171
Woodbridge, VA 22195-6171

Email:

missionarychambers56@gmail.com

www.ingramcontent.com/pod-product-compliance
Lightning Source LLC
Chambersburg PA
CBHW071148090426
42736CB00012B/2269